Contents

CONSIDER HIM

CONSIDER HIM

by

J. Oswald Sanders

MOODY PRESS
CHICAGO

Library of Congress Cataloging in Publication Data
Sanders, John Oswald, 1902-
Consider Him.

Large print ed.
1. Jesus Christ—Meditations. 2. Sight-saving books. I. Ti-
tle.
[BT306.4.S24 1976]   232   76-15012
ISBN 0-8024-1613-6

Printed in the United States of America

Consider Christ

Consider . . . Christ Jesus
(Hebrews 3:1).
Consider him that endured
(Hebrews 12:3).

Two different Greek words are rendered *consider* in these verses in Hebrews. The first carries the idea of the prolonged, concentrated gaze of the astronomer. The second means to reckon up, to compare, or to weigh. Taken together and in their context, these words are an exhortation to consciously fix our minds on

Christ, comparing and weighing His sorrows and sufferings and testings with our own. What was the secret of His serenity? This contemplation of Christ is here presented as a panacea for our spiritual maladies.

It will cure our self-satisfaction. Do we compare ourselves favorably with others? Do we criticize their actions and attitudes? Criticism is always made from a position of superiority. But instead of comparing ourselves with others, we should be comparing ourselves with Him who did no sin. Self-satisfaction withers in the presence of the selfless Christ.

It will deliver us from self-pity. This is a spiritual disease to which we all

8

are too prone. Too many are vocally sorry for themselves and feel that life has given them a raw deal. They feel misunderstood and neglected. "Consider him that endured" (12:3). Was He misunderstood, badly treated, unappreciated, misjudged? He knew what it was to be misjudged by His family. Compared with His, our trials are trivial.

It is the antidote for discouragement. "Consider Him . . . lest ye be wearied and faint in your minds" (v. 3). Aristotle used the word *wearied* to describe an athlete who throws himself down utterly exhausted after winning the race. Discouragement is one of Satan's most debilitating weapons. If we withstand his other wiles, he will attack us here. "Consider him that endured." He was despised, rejected, and maligned. His ministry was not conspicuously successful. His own intimates doubted, denied, forsook Him. Yet He endured. Consider Him, and take heart again.

It will prove a stimulant for lethargy. "Ye have not yet resisted unto blood, striving against sin" (v. 4). Have we grown lethargic in the battle against sin in our own lives and in the lives of others? Never for one moment did Christ relax in His warfare with Satan until He dismissed His spirit on the cross.

It is a remedy for forgetfulness. "Ye

have forgotten the exhortation" (v. 5). Have we forgotten the purpose of our Father's chastening? Let us neither despise nor faint under it, but embrace it in the confidence that afterward it will produce a rich harvest (v. 11).

The Infant Christ

*That holy thing which shall be born of
thee shall be called the Son of God*
(Luke 1:35).

"There is a new baby born every
minute. What is unique about this
one?" The shepherds and the Magi
might have said this about the baby
Jesus. But they didn't. They wor-
shiped Him, while a multitude of the
heavenly host praised God for His
unspeakable gift.

This baby was unique in many
ways. He was the only baby *whose*

conception was not the beginning of His existence. He claimed, "Before Abraham was, I am" (John 8:58). How could there be an incarnation if there had been no previous existence? To deny the latter makes the former impossible. To go back further, could there be a Trinity if there were no pre-existent Son of God? Jesus was unique among men because His birth did not mark His origin.

He was the only baby *who had no human father.* He was conceived by the supernatural operation of the Holy Spirit. "The Holy Ghost shall come upon thee, and the power of the Highest shall overshadow thee," were the angel's words to Mary in Luke 1:35. It had taken more than four millenniums for God to prepare for this momentous event. Was His birth likely to be according to the ordinary course of nature? A person such as Jesus demanded a birth such as Scripture records.

No other baby was *born without taint of sin.* "That holy thing which shall be born of thee shall be called the Son of God." He was holy, harmless, undefiled—free from all moral impurity. Fearlessly He challenged His contemporaries: "Which one of you convicts Me of sin?" (John 8:46, NASB). John's testimony was, "In him is no sin" (1 John 3:5).

He was the only baby *who was more than man.* He possessed two natures—Son of Man and Son of God—and yet united, and functioning in a single personality. "He continueth to be God and Man, in two distinct natures and one person for ever" (Westminster Catechism). Is this mysterious? Yes! "Without controversy great is the mystery of godliness: . . . God was manifest in the flesh" (1 Timothy 3:16).

Finally, He was the only baby *who was born for the purpose of dying.* To all others death was inevitable. To Him it was self-chosen.

No wonder that two millenniums later, the whole world stops to take

notice of His birthday, and that so
much beloved music is devoted to
His unique birth.

The Face of Christ

*The light of the knowledge of the glory
of God in the face of Jesus Christ*
(2 Corinthians 4:6).

How expressive the face is! It mirrors the changing emotions of the soul. It is the index to character and personality. It reveals both weaknesses and strengths. It betrays sorrow or joy, hatred or love, cruelty or sympathy.

Our Lord's face was entirely different from anything any artist has portrayed on canvas. It was absolutely unique because it reflected not only Himself but His Father—*the glory of God* in the face of Jesus Christ. "He that hath seen me hath seen the Father" (John 14:9). But when sinful men saw the glory, they extinguished it.

The face of Jesus Christ revealed *the holiness of God.* "His head and His hair were white like white wool, like snow" (Revelation 1:14, NASB). Our faces carry the lines of sin, but in Him is no sin. In His case, the transmission of the racial heritage was interrupted by the virgin birth. He knew sin only by seeing it in others and by suffering for it. His face reflected the purity of His heart.

It revealed *the steadfastness of God.* "He steadfastly set his face to go to Jerusalem" (Luke 9:51). The Samaritans recognized the marks of resolution on His face, and how greatly He needed it. The road from Bethlehem to Golgotha was rock-strewn and steeply uphill. Many things could deter and deflect Him and weaken His resolve, but He steadfastly held His course.

The sympathy of God was etched on His face. "He beheld the city, and wept over it" (Luke 19:41). What a concept—a weeping God! The glory of God was expressed in salty tears coursing down the face of the Son of Man! He envisaged the scene, still forty years distant, when blood would flow like water in Jerusalem's streets.

It manifested *the wrath of God.* He "looked round about on them with anger, being grieved for the hardness of their hearts" (Mark 3:5). The face of Christ blazed with holy anger! Does this seem incongruous? Is He not "gentle Jesus, meek and mild"? Scripture reveals that Jesus was capable of burning indignation, but it was the wrath of love. *Grieved* is a word that is used only of one who loves.

His face expressed *the gladness of God.* "His face did shine as the sun" (Matthew 17:2). It was not sad and hopeless, but radiant. His injunction,

"Be not . . . of a sad countenance" (Matthew 6:16), tacitly implies that His own face reflected the joy of God.

The Head of Christ

On his head were many crowns
(Revelation 19:12).

The head is the control-tower of the body. From it impulses and messages are transmitted to the farthest limb. It is the dominant part of the body. Our Lord's head is mentioned several times in Scripture, sometimes in its humiliation, sometimes in its exaltation.

His was *a homeless head.* "The Son of man hath not where to lay his head" (Luke 9:58). In these graphic words Jesus indicated His rejection by His people. There was no bed for Him in the inn. Many was the night His head never touched a pillow. During His ministry, He had no home and was dependent on the hospitality of others.

But it was also *an anointed head.* In the extravagance of her love, Mary broke the priceless box of fragrant anointing oil and poured it over His head (Mark 14:3). Her act of love was to Him a green oasis in the dreary desert of rejection, a refrshing draught on the desolate road to the cross. Not everyone rejected Him.

His head was *callously struck by His tormentors.* "They . . . took the reed, and smote Him on the head" (Matthew 27:30). The reed, mock royal sceptre, was used to bruise and degrade the head of the Son of God. "He was bruised for our iniquities" (Isaiah 53:5). And those who struck Him were representative of us all.

His head was *crowned in mockery*. (Matthew 27:29). Thorns, symbol of the curse, adorned the brow of the Lord of glory, every thorn a point of fire.

> Is there diadem, as monarch,
> That His brow adorns?
> "Yea, a crown, in very surety,
> But of thorns."
> —AUTHOR UNKNOWN

"He bowed his head, and gave up the ghost" (John 19:30). All through the ghastly ordeal of crucifixion, His head had remained erect. The curse broke His heart but did not bow His head. Now His work was finished.

Again we see His head *in dazzling majesty.* "His head . . . as white as snow" (Revelation 1:14). It is again erect and radiant. Never again will He bow it before His creatures. In His hand there is no longer a mocking reed, but the scepter of universal dominion.

Our final view of His head is *crowned with many crowns* (Revelation 19:12). He is crowned with glory and honor, the reward of His obedience unto death.

The Hands of Christ

He lifted up His hands, and blessed them (Luke 24:50).

Like our faces, our hands reveal much to the intelligent observer. How expressive they are—an index to our character and habits. With practiced discipline we can mask our facial expression, but how are we to mask our hands? They tell their own story. They can beckon or repulse. They can caress or kill. They can be inexpressibly tender or diabolically cruel.

What has Scripture to say about the hands of our Lord? First, that they were *human hands* (Luke 24:39-40). To the beleaguered and frightened disciples in the upper room, the risen Christ suddenly appeared. Their fears were dispelled when He said to them, "Behold my hands." The livid nail-marks forever assured them that He was the very same Jesus they had known before His crucifixion.

They were *stainless hands*. "Who shall ascend into the hill of the LORD?" asked the psalmist. "He that hath clean hands," was the reply (24:3-4). Christ's hands were never stained by a single sin. They never performed an action contrary to His Father's will.

They were *calloused hands*. "What mighty works are wrought by his hands? Is not this the carpenter?" (Mark 6:2-3). He came to earth as a working man and demonstrated the dignity of honest labor. Jesus sweated at a carpenter's bench, placing Himself on the level of the laborer.

Then they were *sympathetic hands*. "Jesus . . . put forth his hand and touched him" (Mark 1:41). Unafraid of contagion, Jesus gave the amazed leper the touch of human compassion he had been denied for so long.

They were *wounded hands*. "What

are these wounds in thine hands?" was the probing question of Zechariah 13:6. The reply: "Those with which I was wounded in the house of my friends." How eloquent of love and mercy were the prints of the nails.

Then, too, they were *powerful hands*. He "meted out the heavens with the span" (Isaiah 40:12). The limitless oceans lie as a drop in His palm. They were *uplifted in blessing* (Luke 24:50). Our last glimpse of the Master before His ascension is with His powerful hands spread in blessing.

They are *protecting hands*. "Neither shall any man pluck them out of my

hand" (John 10:28). How utterly safe
we are!

The Suffering Christ

Christ also suffered for us, leaving us an example (1 Peter 2:21).

Our Lord was the Prince of sufferers. Here, as in all else, He was preeminent. We tend to conceive of His sufferings mainly in the realm of the physical, but so intense were His spiritual sufferings that physical pain could have been almost a relief.

He was *a sinless Sufferer.* Note the juxtaposition of the two thoughts: Christ "suffered for us, . . . who did no sin" (1 Peter 2:21-22). His sin-

lessness only added to the poignancy of His sufferings. Suffering can mean much or little according to the nature of the person. An unmusical person does not perceive a discord, but to the sensitive musician it causes exquisite pain. Neglect is not keenly felt when love is lacking. In the human nature of the Master, passion had not done its ugly work, nor had His powers become atrophied through neglect. It is the holy person who feels sin most keenly.

He was *a sensitive Sufferer.* Jesus was the essence of refinement and sensitivity. He possessed all the gentler graces as well as all the virility of manhood. He was by nature a sensitive person. How He must have suffered when denounced as a deceiver and a liar (John 7:12); a blasphemer (Matthew 9:3); in league with the devil (John 8:52); a glutton and a drunkard (Luke 7:34). Jesus was really human, and these charges occasioned Him intense suffering. His suffering was real, not a theatrical display; and these verbal barbs pierced more deeply than the crown of thorns.

He was *a sacrificial Sufferer.* The substitutionary element in Christ's death is prominent in this paragraph. "Christ suffered for us . . . who his own self bare our sins in his own body on the tree" (1 Peter 2:21, 24).

He not only pardoned our sins but took them away. How amazing that the blood that stained the soldier's spear was the sole remedy for the soldier's sin! Whoever dreamed of the crime procuring the salvation? And His death was not only vicarious but voluntary. He was led, not dragged to the cross.

He was *a silent Sufferer.* "When he was reviled, reviled not again" (1 Peter 2:23). He harbored no spirit of retaliation. Like an aromatic leaf, the crushing only released the fragrance. Not a word of complaint crossed His lips. Instead He "committed himself to him that judgeth righteously" (1 Peter 2:23).

The Crucified Christ

They crucified him (John 19:18).

Christ was unique in His death as in His birth. In a perceptive and picturesque statement of a great truth, Martin Niemoller said, "The cradle and the cross of Christ were hewn from the same tree." The incarnation was solely with a view to the crucifixion.

Our Lord's death was unique in that it was *the only death that fulfilled millenniums of prophecy.* The sufferings and death of the Messiah were not only foreshadowed in meticulous detail in the Jewish sacrificial system, but they were foretold by the prophets. It has been stated that even in His tragic hours on the cross, thirty-three separate Old Testament prophecies were fulfilled.

He was *the only Person to whom death was not inevitable.* "I lay down my life. . . . No man taketh it from me, but I lay it down of myself" (John 10:17-18). To Him, death was deliberately chosen. He "gave himself for us," wrote Paul to Titus (2:14). He was not dragged to the cross, but drawn by quenchless love.

To Him alone, *death was not a result of sin.* "The wages of sin is death" (Romans 6:23); but as He did no sin,

He did not need to collect its wages. This left Him perfectly free to assume the burden and guilt of the world's sin and to provide deliverance from its bondage.

His was *the only death accompanied by miracles.* It was appropriate that a life replete with miracles should conclude with a series of miracles. There was the mysterious darkness which was no eclipse, since the moon was then at its farthest from the sun. And it lasted not for a few minutes but for three hours.

There was the miraculous rending of the veil, sixty feet long and thirty feet wide, requiring three hundred men to handle it. The rent was from top to bottom, by no human hand. A mighty earthquake accompanied His death. Rocks were rent, and graves opened. "Many bodies of the saints which slept arose . . . and appeared to many" (Matthew 27:52-53), conclusive evidence of His power over death.

Finally, His was *the only death that made possible the forgiveness of sins*—an experience to which myriads can testify.

> When Thou didst hang upon the tree
> The quaking earth acknowldged Thee
> When Thou didst there yield up Thy breath
> The world grew dark as shades of death.
>
> —AUTHOR UNKNOWN

The Risen Christ

Christ died for our sins; . . . he was buried, . . . he rose again the third day (1 Corinthians 15:3-4).

These verses enshrine the essence of the Christian faith. They contain the essential message of Easter, the most important event in the church year. Three great truths are emphasized. On Friday Jesus died on the cross. On Saturday He lay in Joseph's tomb. On Sunday He rose from the dead. Deny these fundamental facts and you negate Christianity.

45

Two other very important things about Christ emerge from these verses. First, *He was truly man* because He died. Death is characteristic of mankind. In this fact lay the necessity for the incarnation. *He was also really God* because He rose from the dead. Man cannot rise from the dead. Because Jesus was infinite, His death was of infinite value and made expiation for the sins of the whole world.

Exactly in the manner and for the purposes revealed in the Scriptures, He died for our sins. He was buried, not in a common grave, but in a new tomb. *He rose again* on the third day under the circumstances recorded in Scripture. It was *a bodily resurrection.*

When the women and Peter and John looked into the tomb, it was empty except for the graveclothes, still lying in the folds that had encased Him. The butterfly had flown, leaving an empty chrysallis.

Muslims glory in a full coffin in Mecca. Christians glory in an empty tomb in Jerusalem. We have a living Christ; they have a dead prophet.

But how can the resurrection be explained? Christ's body must have been removed either by human or by superhuman hands. If by human hands, it must have been by the hands of friends or foes. His foes would not, because that would look as if He really had risen. His friends could not remove the body for the tomb was sealed, and a guard of sixty soldiers watched to ensure that it was not rifled. The only alternative is that "God the Father . . . raised him from the dead" (Galatians 1:1).

If Christ did not rise from the dead as His disciples claimed, we cannot account for the complete transformation of these men who had been cowering behind closed doors for fear of the Jews. Their radiant joy and fearless witness is testimony of His transformation.

> You ask me how I know He lives?
> He lives within my heart.
> A. H. ACKLEY

The Ascended Christ

*He was parted from them, and carried
up into heaven* (Luke 24:51).

The ascension of our Lord directs
attention to the fact that He is not
only risen, but *enthroned*. It is that
event in which the risen Christ finally
and visibly withdrew from His disciples and passed into the heavens—a
fitting climax to His life of perfect
obedience on earth. His glorious ascension was the necessary and appropriate complement to His resur-

rection, and the manner in which it took place was consistent with His miraculous life and achievements.

He did not vanish out of sight as He did at Emmaus (Luke 24:31) leaving a question as to whether there might be yet further appearances. He walked away from them, and then He was carried up into heaven, there to sit at the right hand of God. It took place as they were looking on, in broad daylight (Acts 1:9). There was no possibility of mistake. He was really and finally gone.

He ascended bodily, and carried His glorified human body into heaven. He left them, *with His hands outstretched in blessing.* As soon as His nail-pierced feet left the earth, He commenced His ministry as their Advocate and Intercessor. They exchanged His physical presence for His spiritual omnipresence.

The ascension was an important part of the Lord's ministry on our behalf. It imparted *the assurance that His death was effective* and that all God's claims against sinful men had been met. It evidenced the fact that the problem created by man's sin had been finally solved. It enabled His disciples to give a satisfying account of the disappearance of Christ's body from the tomb.

Further, it was *the necessary prelude to the coming of the Holy Spirit* as promised by the Lord. Hitherto "the Spirit was not yet given, because Jesus was not yet glorified" (John 7:39, NASB). Now the way was open for the Pentecostal effusion. By the ascension, the local Christ became the universal Christ whose personal presence was mediated by the Holy Spirit.

To Christ, it was *the reward of His obedience* unto death. "Therefore also God highly exalted Him" (Philippians 2:9, NASB). The ascension reversed man's verdict on the Son of God.

Had the Saviour not ascended, we would be without a representative in heaven, and without the Comforter to lead and guide us on earth. His presence in heaven makes heaven a blessed reality to us.

The Returning Christ

I will come again (John 14:3).

The return of Christ to earth is the denouement toward which the Church has been looking for centuries. Our salvation is "nearer now than when we first believed" (Romans 13:11), and so is the second advent of our Lord. It is not only the object of our anticipation, but of admonition to very practical Christian duties. A careful study will reveal that this event is linked to every great doctrine and ethical duty.

It sounds *a call to consecration*. "Behold, I am coming like a thief. Blessed is the one who stays awake, and keeps his garments" (Revelation 16:15, NASB). We are to be punctilious in keeping the garments of the soul stainless. Are we as careful in this realm as we are of the garments we wear?

When others see our garments, they see us. We are to "put on Christ" (Galatians 3:27), so that others will see Him when they see us. In these Laodicean days our Lord counsels us to "buy of me . . . white raiment that thou mayest be clothed" (Revelation 3:18).

His return carries with it *the assur-*

ance of reward. "Behold I come quickly; and my reward is with me" (Revelation 22:12). There is a tendency to regard the reward motive as a commercializing of Christianity, but it played a prominent part in the thinking of the early Church. Paul frequently refers to it, as did his Master.

Some Christians piously protest that they will be content with the lowest place in heaven, but this is false humility and could be a cloak for spiritual lethargy. "So run, that ye may obtain" the promised reward (1 Corinthians 9:24). In any case, rewards are not *given,* they are *earned.*

Heavenly rewards are for earthly renunciations.

The second advent is *an encouragement to continuance.* "Behold I come quickly: hold that fast which thou hast, that no man take thy crown" (Revelation 3:11).

In Hebrews 2:1 we are exhorted not to drift away from the truth we have heard. The ascended Lord urges us to hold fast what we already have, lest our reward be taken by someone else. His imminent return provides the motive for this.

There may still be years before this blessed hope is realized. Let us fill the days with sacrificial service. Spiritual indolence means eternal loss.

The Unchanging Christ

Jesus Christ the same yesterday, and to day, and for ever (Hebrews 13:8).

No one can doubt that we are living in a changing world. Indeed, the rate of change in every realm of life is so rapid that we find it impossible to keep pace with its kaleidoscopic movements. H. F. Lyte's hymn is more appropriate today than when he wrote it:

Change and decay in all around I see,
O Thou who changest not, abide with me.

In the midst of our changing and unstable world stands the unchanging Christ. In Hebrews 13:7, the writer exhorts Christians to remember their former teachers; but in verse 8, he turns their eyes to Jesus, who is always the same. All that He was in the past, He is in the present and will be in the future.

Jesus Christ, *the same yesterday,* will care for all our yesterdays. Our past sometimes haunts and even paralyzes us, and the devil delights to keep us chained to it. But the changeless Christ is able to cleanse us from all the guilt and defilement of the past. He is able to deliver us even from the tyranny of memory. We must not allow the devil to resurrect what God has forgotten. We should remember, too, that for the believer He is the God of the second chance. "I am the LORD, I change not; therefore ye . . . are not consumed" (Malachai 3:6).

Jesus Christ, *the same today,* will take care of all our todays. He who delivers from the tyranny of the past will dissolve the perplexities of the present. And how insoluble they often seem—cares of family, health, finance, business, age. But no problem is really new; they are common to all ages. Jesus experienced family problems. He had no money to pay His tax. He wept in sorrow with Mary. He can solve temperamental problems as He did with Peter. As Great Physician, He can help in our physical problems.

Jesus Christ, *the same for ever,* is well able to care for all our tomorrows. He is able to dispel the uncertainties of the future. We are all apt to succumb to fear. There are fears that assail us at every stage of life. Fear of the future can cripple us in meeting the demands of the present. But in the midst of life's uncertainties stands One who is utterly dependable and entirely competent. *Trust Him fully.*

The Mind of Christ

Let this mind be in you which was also in Christ Jesus (Philippians 2:5).

In this great Christological passage, Paul throws out a startling challenge: Reflect in your own mind the mind of Christ.

The mind of Christ was more than His thinking processes; it was His entire inner disposition. It included His thoughts and motives and desires. Because we reflect the mind of Christ so imperfectly, we make a very slight impression on the cynical world around us. "The world does not believe in Him whom it has not seen, because it has cause not to believe in us whom it has seen" (J. Stuart Holden).

The mind of Christ is seen operating on two levels in this passage.

On the level of deity, Christ did not count equality with God and its attendant majesty something to be retained and grasped at all costs. He did not greedily cling to His rights as God's equal. Instead, He emptied Himself. He resigned all His outward glory, veiled His majesty, and accepted the limitations involved in assuming human form. He could never be less than God, but He renounced the outward display of His majesty and glory. Yielding up the independent exercise of His divine attributes, He became a servant. "Let this mind be in you, which was also in Christ Jesus."

The mind of Christ displayed *on the level of humanity.* "He humbled himself" (v. 8). We have every reason to humble ourselves, but it was not so with Him. He did not demand, as He might well have done, such a standard of treatment as befitted His dignity. Instead of a palace, He chose a manger. His throne was a carpenter's bench, and His sceptre a hammer. His university was a village school. So low did He stoop in His self-humiliation that He accepted the lowest step—death on a cross.

This display of His mind was progressive. It began in His thinking, led to self-abasement, and culminated in self-oblation. Sacrificial love led Him to take these downward steps, and we are to follow His example.

His mind was the exact reverse of the worldly mind that revels in position and power; that considers wealth and possessions the greatest good; that delights in being served rather than in serving others; that shrinks from suffering and shame.

"Let this mind be in you."

The Love of Christ

The love of Christ, . . . passeth knowledge (Ephesians 3:19).

Love expresses itself in a seemingly contradictory way. Parental love expresses itself in a wholesome and loving discipline, not in the indulgence of a child's every whim. But not every child appreciates this expression of love. It is the same with the Lord's children.

In the gospels, three expressions of Christ's love are recorded for our instruction. In each case it is stated

71

that the Lord loved the person involved.

We learn first that *Christ's love corrects* the one whom He loves. Speaking of the young ruler, Mark says, "Then Jesus beholding him loved him" (10:21). And what did His love move Him to do? Jesus saw that the young man had many attractive qualities, but he lacked the greatest essential. He discerned the fatal flaw in the life of the ruler and dealt faithfully with him about it. Alas, in clinging to his great possessions, he sacrificed the greatest Possession.

So will our divine Lord put His unerring finger on our fatal flaw, the thing that will rob us of His highest blessings. Shall we ask Him to show us what that thing is?

Next we see that *Christ's love allows suffering* by His loved ones. "Now Jesus loved Martha, and her sister [Mary], and Lazarus" (John 11:5). Jesus spent more time in their home than in any other. Was He soft and indulgent with this favored family? No, He was not. He did not intervene to prevent Lazarus traversing the vale of death. He did not spare the sisters the heartbreak of seeing him slowly slip away. Rather, He waited two days before responding to their appeal for help. Did He not care? He cared so much that He permitted their suffering.

74

And what was His purpose? "To the intent that ye may believe" (v. 15). The cultivation of faith was the object of the discipline. After their trial, they had an immeasurably greater Lord, and their suffering has been used to impart comfort and insight to succeeding generations of believers.

Last, *Christ's love cleanses.* "Having loved his own . . . [he] began to wash the disciples feet" (John 13:1, 5). At that moment, He was on His way to cleanse their defiled souls with His blood, but He paused to give a matchless demonstration of the humility of love. No task is too menial for love. Jesus washed their feet with water, and then with blood from the basin of the cross.

The Meekness of Christ

I am meek and lowly in heart
(Matthew 11:29).

In these words, Jesus crowned the modest grace of meekness queen of virtues. In the Lord's time, as in our own, meekness was regarded as anything but a virtue. A meek person was regarded as effeminate and servile. Do we not usually associate the word with someone who is insignificant and labors under an inferiority complex?

The word was one of the great ethical words of the Greeks. Aristotle viewed it as the happy mean between two extremes: between too much anger and too little anger, for example. It was also used of the breaking-in of a horse in which the animal learned to accept control and bow to the will of another. With this background, let us consider its application to the Lord.

It might be said that meekness plus lowliness equals humility. Meekness is humility toward God. Lowliness is humility toward men. Jesus claimed both qualities for Himself. From this it is clear that meekness is not the equivalent of weakness or mildness of disposition. His activity in cleansing the Temple was anything but mild. Meekness is strong, but it is strength held in control. When the glory of God is involved, the meek person can fight with vigor.

In what ways did Jesus display this lowly grace? *He demonstrated it in His boyhood* when, after His experience in the Temple, he went home and was subject to his parents (Luke 2:41-52).

Without complaint *He was willing to perform the lowliest duties.* He made ploughs and yokes for the farmers of Nazareth. What an occupation for Him who made the worlds! He meekly accepted the Father's plan for His life, even though it involved exchanging the freedom of the universe for the restrictions of a village carpenter's shop.

Jesus was meek in His dealings with failing mortals—with doubting Thomas, with traitorous Judas, with denying Peter, with the adulterous woman.

Meekness is essentially *the attitude that does not insist on its own rights,* but is always ready to waive privilege in the interests of others. Is this grace prominent in our lives? Meekness is measured by what we can endure without complaint or retaliation or demanding our rights. The meek person is acquiescent to the will of God.

How can we learn this grace of meekness? "The fruit of the Spirit is . . . meekness" (Galatians 5:22-23).

The Humility of Christ

He humbled Himself (Philippians 2:8).

To His ambitious disciples Jesus said, "I am among you as He that serveth" (Luke 22:27). The background of this staggering assertion was the unseemly strife among His disciples as to who should be greatest in His kingdom. With such a sordid backdrop, the Master's humility stands in striking contrast.

Humility is a distinctively human

grace, though Christ's contemporaries viewed it as anything but a virtue. He ennobled the word and invested it with new meaning. Humility is not, as many feel, thinking meanly of oneself. Rather, it is thinking not of oneself at all! This was characteristic of our Lord. To Him, humility was not a Sunday frock, but a workday smock. He was clothed with humility; and it was not a temporary pose, but a life disposition.

Let us consider first *the example He set*. It has rightly been said that He was a standing rebuke to pride of every kind, and a living example of humility at its highest. By working as a carpenter, He rebuked pride of birth and of rank. He rebuked the pride of independence by allowing women to supply His financial needs. He rebuked pride of intellect when He said, "As my Father hath taught me, I speak these things" (John 8:28). He rebuked pride of ability when He asserted, "The Son can do nothing of himself" (John 5:19). He was content to be nothing, in order that His Father might be all.

Notice how often He used *nothing* and *not* of Himself in John's gospel? Underline the occurrences and then follow the example. Jesus was just as humble before men as He was before God.

And what of *the teaching He gave* on

this theme? His humility consisted in the surrender of Himself to God for the fulfillment of His will, and He taught us to have the same attitude.

Hear His words. "Blessed are the poor in spirit" (Matthew 5:3). "Learn of me; for I am meek and lowly in heart" (Matthew 11:29). "He that humbleth himself shall be exalted" (Luke 14:11). "Whosoever will be chief, let him be the servant of all" (Matthew 20:27).

Only the indwelling Christ can make us truly humble and self-forgetful; only He can reproduce in us His own humility. How slow we are to learn that *God's way up is down!* Our pride derived from the first Adam, but the sole source of our humility is the Second Adam.

The Preciousness of Christ

Unto you therefore which believe he is precious (1 Peter 2:7).

As a lad of sixteen, the celebrated Charles Haddon Spurgeon preached his first sermon from this text. Could he have chosen a text more spacious and limitless to a lover of Christ?

Christ was *precious to God.* "I was daily his delight" (Proverbs 8:30). "This is my beloved Son in whom I am well pleased," was God's testimony at Jesus' baptism (Matthew

3:17). He was inexpressibly dear to His Father. Everything in His walk from Bethlehem to Calvary gave Him infinite delight.

Since this is so, it is little wonder that He is *precious to the believer.* It should be noted that here the word *precious* (in 1 Peter 2:7). is a noun, not an adjective. It could be better rendered, "Unto you that believe He is the preciousness;" that is, preciousness itself. An adjective admits of degrees, but not a noun. To the believer He is the essence of all preciousness.

All the most precious things are hid in Him—"all the treasures of wisdom and knowledge" (Colossians 2:3), "all

the fullness of the Godhead bodily"
(2:9). We may lose any of earth's precious things, but we can never lose Jesus, our priceless treasure. Even death serves only to bring Him nearer. He is a jewel of which neither Satan nor death can rob us. Heat can destroy even a diamond, but the fiercest heat of trial cannot separate the believer from Christ. He shares our sorrows, lightens our loads, and doubles our joys.

He is the *cornerstone of our faith* "disallowed indeed of men, but chosen of God, and precious" (1 Peter 2:4).

He is *precious as Saviour.* He not only saves us from our sin, but shares

His own life with us. Should this not make Him inexpressibly precious to us?

It is when we are in deepest need that we most appreciate His preciousness. He is the complement to our every need. Charles H. Spurgeon enshrined this truth in a hymn:

What the hand is to the lute,
What the breath is to the flute,
What is fragrance to the smell,
What the spring is to the well,
What the flower is to the bee,
That is Jesus Christ to me.

What the mother to the child,
What the guide in pathless wild,
What is oil to troubled wave,
What is ransom to the slave,
What is water to the sea,
That is Jesus Christ to me.

The Power of Christ

The power of Christ . . . dwell in me
(2 Corinthians 12:9, NASB).

It is a truth of Scripture that whatever Christ is, He is for us by virtue of our vital union with Him. He is the reservoir of divine omnipotence, from which we can constantly draw for our ever-recurring needs.

It is instructive to note that the Greek word *dunamis*, or inherent power, is different from *exousia,* or authority. *Exousia* is never predicated of our Lord by the evangelists. Nor in the Scripture record does He claim its exercise. There is only one occasion on which both words are used of Him: "What a word is this! for with authority and power he commandeth the unclean spirits, and they come out" (Luke 4:36). But these were the words of neither the evangelist nor of Jesus, but of the spectators. Elsewhere, only *exousia*, authority, is used of Him. "All authority has been given to Me in heaven and on earth" (Matthew 28:18, NASB).

Jesus was the Son of God, but He completely identified Himself with the human race. Therefore, in fulfilling His earthly ministry, He never exercised or drew on His *inherent power,* but exerted only the *authority delegated* from His Father.

There is much comfort and encouragement for us ordinary mortals in this fact. When we read of Christ's miraculous works of power, it does not help us much. We say, "Yes, that is wonderful, but He was the Son of God. I am just a frail and erring man. Christ had powers and resources that are not available to me. He was sinless and I am sinful."

But that is just where we are wrong. Although He possessed limitless inherent power, He voluntarily refrained from using it. In order that He might be made "in all things . . .

like unto His brethren" (Hebrews 2:17), He renounced that privilege, and restricted Himself to exercise only the authority His Father had delegated to Him. "I can of mine own self do nothing," was His astounding claim.

His miracles were not performed by innate power, but in dependence upon the Holy Spirit. In the same way, the miracles wrought by the apostles were done by the authority He delegated to them.

So instead of being discouraged by the fact that He was the Son of God, we can be encouraged that He chose to be continually dependent on His Father for power to do His will.

The Lordship of Christ

*To this end Christ both died and rose
. . . that he might be Lord*
(Romans 14:9).

Paul claims here that our Lord died and came to life again for one main purpose—to establish His lordship over dead and living. This is in keeping with the crucial sentence of the Pentecostal sermon: "God hath made that same Jesus . . . both Lord and Christ" (Acts 2:36). We must emphasize that the Christ who died for

us lives to rule in the lives of those He has redeemed.

It is tragic that *while many Christians verbally acknowledge Christ's Lordship, they do not concede it to Him in practice.* They are willing to accord Him the position of constitutional Monarch, so long as they can remain prime minister. Like Peter, they reserve the right to say, "Not so, Lord" (Acts 10:14).

Do we ever say "not so" to Him? He moves us to pray in prayer meetings, but we say "not so, Lord." He calls us to service, or witness, and we say "Not so." To such Jesus says, "Why call ye me Lord, Lord, and do not the things which I say?" (Luke 6:46).

It is not possible to accept Christ as Saviour and to reject Him as Lord. He cannot be divided. We cannot accept Him in one office and reject Him in another. Hudson Taylor was right when he said, "If He is not Lord of all, He is not Lord at all." A. W. Tozer with his usual pungency said, "It is altogether doubtful whether any man can be saved who comes to Christ for His help, but with no intention of obeying Him."

Christ's reign in our hearts is very practical and extends to every area of life. *Disobedience vitiates all our pious professions of recognition of His Lord-*

ship. The test is not what we say, but what we do. What we perform always speaks more loudly than what we profess.

Isaiah puts the situation very tersely "O LORD our God, other masters than thou have ruled us, but through Thee alone we confess Thy name" (26:13, NASB).

How can we acknowledge His Lordship? We must do the following: (1) make a break with the past and vow that other lords shall no longer rule; (2) decisively renounce all known sin or disobedience; (3) enthrone Christ alone, and refuse to acknowledge any other name; (4) depend on the Holy Spirit—"no man can say that Jesus is Lord, but by the Holy Ghost" (1 Corinthians 12:3).

Union with Christ

*Know ye not that your bodies are
the members of Christ?*
(1 Corinthians 6:15).

One of the most important doctrines relating to the inner spiritual life of the believer is that of his vital union with Christ. Indeed it could be claimed that it is our only hope of victory over sin, and of triumph in the testing circumstances of life. Yet many Christians do not know that they have been grafted into Christ and that they are vitally united to

Him. As a result of this union, every-thing He achieved by His life and death becomes ours.

Several figures are used in Scripture to illustrate this mystical union. There is *the figure of marriage:* "that ye should be married to another, even to him who is raised from the dead" (Romans 7:4). This is the highest and most intimate union known to man, and is a picture of Christ and His Church. (Ephesians 5:31, 32).

There is *the figure of the body and the head.* "Know ye not that your bodies are members of Christ?" "Grow up into Him . . . which is the head, . . . from whom the whole body . . . grows" (Ephesians 4:15).

The picture here is of mutual dependence through sharing the same life. The smallest member of the body shares the life of the head.

Jesus employed *the figure of the vine and the branches.* "I am the vine, ye are the branches" (John 15:5). The vine and the branches are one. Neither can exist independently of the other, but it is the vine that supplies the vital sap to the branches for fruitbearing. The sole responsibility of the branch is to receive from root and stem the vital, nourishing fluid. Then fruitbearing is automatic.

To Hudson Taylor, at a time when he was heavily burdened, the fact of the union of the believer with Christ as illustrated in the vine and the branches brought a transformation of experience. Here are his own words: "Here I feel is the secret. Not asking how I am to get the sap out of the vine into myself, but remembering that Jesus *is* the Vine—root, stem, branches, leaves, twigs, flowers, fruit. Let us not want to get anything *out* of Him, but rejoice in ourselves being *in* Him. I have not got to make myself a branch. The Lord tells me I *am* a branch. I am part of Him and have just to believe and act on it."

Christ All in All

Christ is all, and in all
(Colossians 3:11).

Paul compresses into these six words his comprehensive creed. They enshrine all the excellencies of Christ. J. B. Phillips gives us the happy rendering, "Christ is all that matters."

The Colossian letter aims primarily at the exaltation of Christ in His personal glory. Of the ninety-five verses in this epistle, Christ is mentioned in eighty. The Colossian Christians were being lured away by the ambitious Gnostic speculations. Paul directs their attention to Jesus alone as the source of fullness of blessing.

He tells them that *in Christ dwells all the fullness of the Godhead* in bodily form (2:9).

> In Him most perfectly expressed,
> The Father's glories shine,
> Of the full Deity possessed
> Eternally divine.
> —AUTHOR UNKNOWN

Christ is the complete embodiment of all there is in God. In this one statement Paul demolished the Docetic heresy which maintained that Christ had no real body, and the Cerinthian heresy which separated the man Jesus from the Christ.

112

He is the all in all of creation. "By him were all things created" (1:16). "All things" here means the whole universe. Ours is a Christocentric universe. He is its nerve center. Paul is underlining the central activity of Christ in creation. The whole creation is designed to reveal Him. The natural shows forth the spiritual.

Christ is the all in all of providence. "He is before all things, and by Him all things consist" (1:17). Christ occupies the whole sphere of human life and permeates all its developments. Nature is not a mechanical automation. Its laws are formulated and administered by the risen Christ. It is by Him that all things cohere, hold together, and "in Him we live, and move, and have our being" (Acts 17:28).

He is the all in all of redemption. "In whom we have redemption through His blood" (Colossians 1:11). He alone has redeemed us. He discharged the debt of our sin, weighing out the ransom price, not in silver or gold, but in crimson drops of precious blood. Jesus nailed the receipted bill to His cross, thus canceling out the bond that was against us (2:14).

At the same time He gloriously defeated the devil and held him up to public disgrace (2:15).

Christ is all that matters.

Christ, Center of Everything

Remember always, as the center of everything, Jesus Christ
(2 Timothy 2:8, Phillips).

In the midst of wise counsel to the young pastor, Paul injects this pungent exhortation. Only as he heeds it will Timothy be able to keep his priorities right. We, too, do well to observe it. The risen Christ is center of everything, for Christianity *is* Christ.

He is *central in history,* for in a very real sense history is *His story.* Time is

divided by His birth. The course of world history has been irrevocably altered by His presence on earth. If Christ is omitted, history does not make sense. He is ignored by the one hundred and thirty nations of the United Nations, yet He controls the destiny and sways the future of them all.

Who can deny that He is central *in art?* Traverse the art galleries of the world and note the subject of the greatest paintings. *In literature* He occupies a central role. The greatest *masterpieces of music* found their inspiration in Him. *In architecture,* no structures combine such symmetry, beauty, and grandeur as the buildings erected for His worship.

He is the *center of the human race.*
In Him alone do we find ideal humanity. He revealed in terms of human life the full perfections of Deity.

In many places Scripture introduces Him as the central figure. We see Him first *in the midst of the doctors,* the experts in religious instruction, to learn of His Father's world purpose (Luke 2:42). He is seen *in the midst of sinners,* bringing salvation (John 19:18). He died as a criminal, but it was on the central cross.

He appears *in the midst of the churches* to scrutinize the shining of their lamp of witness (Revelation 1:13). Having triumphed over death,

He now appraises the work and witness of His Church.

Our final glimpse of Him is *in the midst of the throne to rule*, "a Lamb as it had been slain" (Revelation 5:6). Oh what joy to see Him reigning, receiving the homage of the whole redeemed creation, occupying the central theme of the universe!

Surely this must be the climax. But no, there is something more wonderful. "Where two or three are gathered together in my name, *there am I in the midst*" (Matthew 18:20).

"Remember always, as the center of everything, Jesus Christ."

Ambassadors for Christ

Now then we are ambassadors for Christ (2 Corinthians 5:20).

Paul used many metaphors to illustrate the privileged ministry to which God had called him. One of the most impressive is that of ambassador for Christ.

An ambassador is *a diplomatic minister of state of highest rank.* It is rightly considered one of the highest honors any country can bestow on one of its citizens. Paul delighted to use this term of himself. It is told of Dr. John R. Mott, the great religious leader, that he was once offered the post of ambassador of the United States to Japan. In declining the honor, he said to President Coolidge, "Mr. President, since God called me as a student to be His ambassador, my ears have been deaf to all other calls."

An ambassador has both privileges and responsibilities. First, as to privileges, he actually represents his absent king or president, whose honor is in his hands. He does not go abroad at his own expense. All the resources of his country are behind him. He has personal fellowship with and access to his sovereign. While on the nation's business, his personal safety is guaranteed. It is not difficult to relate these privileges to the post of an ambassador for the King of kings.

Then, as to responsibilities, he is required to have no associations, however seemingly innocent, that would in any way compromise his country. He must keep in constant communication with his sovereign. He must live and conduct himself in a manner worthy of the one he represents. He is expected to watch over and protect the interests of fellow-citizens living in the country to which he has been accredited.

He has no right to either add to or subtract from the message of his government but must deliver it intact. Nor need he apologize for his message. He is not expected to originate his own message, but to receive his government's instructions. He is to present his government's viewpoint, not his own. He may persuade, but not dictate.

It is not difficult to make a pertinent application of these responsibilities to the ambassador of Christ. Do we qualify for the post?